PSYCHOLOGY AND COUNSELING GOD'S WAY

PSYCHOLOGY AND COUNSELING GOD'S WAY

Soul Care Givers

DR. DANETTE VERCHER

Library of Congress Control Number: 2019916968
ISBN: Hardcover   978-1-7960-6712-5
               Softcover   978-1-7960-6711-8
               eBook   978-1-7960-6710-1

Print information available on the last page.

Rev. date: 10/22/2019

To order additional copies of this book, contact:
Xlibris
1-888-795-4274
www.Xlibris.com
Orders@Xlibris.com
801876

CONTENTS

STUDY GUIDE FOR
Basic Principles for Counseling African Americans

STUDY GUIDE FOR
Christian Counseling

STUDY GUIDE FOR
Pastoral Counseling

STUDY GUIDE FOR
Premarital Counseling

PSYCHOLOGY AND COUNSELING

TEXTBOOK:
EFFECTIVE BIBLICAL COUNSELING
BY DR. LARRY CRABB

Approved By: Date: Approved By: Date:

___________________________   ___________________________

CHANCELLOR   **_VERCHER_**

"Study to Show Thyself Approved." 2 Timothy 2:15

PSYCHOLOGY AND COUNSELING   8 CREDIT HOURS

TEXTBOOK: EFFECTIVE BIBLICAL COUNSELING
AUTHOR: DR. LARRY CRABB

THE PURPOSE OF THIS STUDY IS TO GIVE THE STUDENT A "HOLISTIC" APPROACH TO THE STUDY OF HUMAN BEHAVIOR, BY STUDYING HUMAN NATURE AND HUMAN MODIFICATION.

STUDENTS WILL BE EXPECTED TO READ EACH CHAPTER AND DO THE EXERCISES IN THE COURSE OUTLINE BY ANSWERING ALL THE QUESTIONS AND FOREWARDING THE ANSWERS TO THE TEACHER FOR GRADING AND TEACHER COMMENTS.

IF ADDITIONAL PAPER IS NEEDED TO COMPLETE THE ANSWERS PLEASE NOTE THE SUBJECT AND PAGE THE ANSWERS ARE PERTAINING TO.

INTRODUCTION
EFFECTIVE BIBLICAL COUNSELING

<u>QUESTIONS:</u>

1. What is Dr. Larry Crabb's purpose in writing this volume?

    ____

    ____

2. What does effective body life produce?

    ____

    ____

3. Effective counseling requires what?

    ____

    ____

4. What are the twofold functions of Christian professionals?
    A.____
    B.____

THREE KINDS OF COUNSELING

1. What are the three kinds of counseling?
    A. ____
    B. ____
    C. ____

PART I

A FEW PRELIMINARIES
CHAPTER ONE

THE GOAL OF COUNSELING: WHAT ARE WE TRYING TO DO?

QUESTIONS:

1. What has the Lord told us about happiness?

2. Trying to find happiness is something like what?

3. What is the twofold function?
    A.
    B.

4. What can we do to be happy?

5. It is our responsibility as fellow members to do what?

6. What is the goal?

<u>QUESTIONS:</u>

1. Christian maturity involves what?

   ____

   ____

2. Fill in the Sketch:

   ____

   ____

   ____

3. All who are justified will one day have no need of glorification? True or False?

   ____

   ____

4. Our past and future depend entirely on god alone. True or False?

   ____

   ____

5. If we add "Over and Up" to the sketch, are we on the right road to obedience? Yes or No?

   ____

   ____

6. What develops Christian maturity?

   ____

   ____

   ____

CHRISTIANITY AND PSYCHOLOGY: ENEMIES OR ALLIES?
CHAPTER TWO

<u>QUESTIONS:</u>

1. The personal problems, which people bring to counselors, are completely unrelated to spiritual issues; what are the concerns?

    ____

    ____

2. What are the four (4) distinct approaches?

    ____

    ____

    ____

    ____

3. What does Transactional Analysis teach?

    ____

    ____

4. Personality roughly corresponds to biblical descriptions of conscience into three (3) parts. What are they?

    ____

    ____

    ____

5. What obscures issues of morality?

    ____

    ____

6. The first job of integrationist is to do what?

    ____

    ____

7. What includes both Theologians and Psychologists and also handles the problem of integration by disregarding psychology altogether?

____

____

8. What two grounds does nothing Butterist Colleagues primarily?

____

____

9. What is the spoiling of the Egyptian?

____

____

10. What was it that the Israelites took with them and shouldn't have?

____

____

11. What is the Santa Claus Theology?

____

____

PERSONAL NEEDS: WHAT DO PEOPLE NEED TO LIVE EFFECTIVELY?
CHAPTER THREE

QUESTIONS:

1. Explain the personal needs of Mr. A, Mrs. B, Mr. C, and Mrs. D.

____

____

____

____

____

____

2. What kind of input do both men and women need?

____

____

____

3. What would be the two required inputs of Adam and Eve and both according to the diagram?

____

____

____

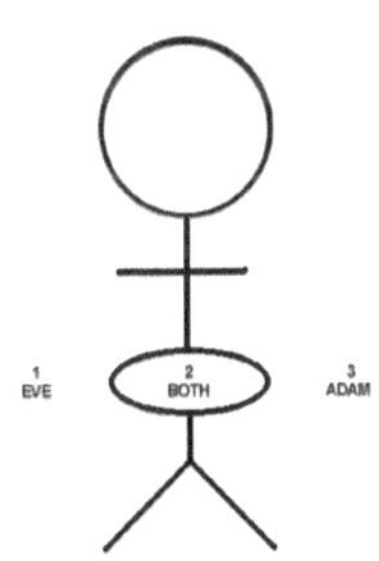

4. What is the question Proverbs 18:14 asks?

    ____

    ____

5. True significance and security are available to everyone: Even if there's no trust in Christ. True or False?

    ____

    ____

6. What are the two basic drives behind human behavior?

    ____

    ____

7. What is Freud's meaning for Thanatos?

    ____

    ____

8. What is our world and country characterized by?

    ____

    ____

9. When did God's judgment fall on Sodom and Gomorrah?

    ____

    ____

10. Explain the diagram on a Christian point of view

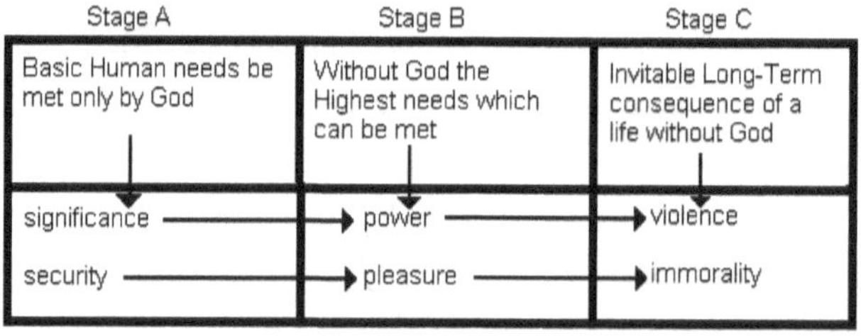

Stage A	Stage B	Stage C
Basic Human needs be met only by God	Without God the Highest needs which can be met	Invitable Long-Term consequence of a life without God
significance →	power →	violence
security →	pleasure →	immorality

    ____

    ____

    ____

    ____

11. Can a Christian repent and return to the true significance and
    security? Yes or No?

    ____

    ____

12. Can anyone move over to Stage B or A?

    ____

    ____

MOTIVATION: WHY DO WE DO WHAT WE DO?
CHAPTER FOUR

<u>QUESTIONS:</u>

1. Why do we do what we do?

2. How many basic propositions are listed?

3. Explain all propositions by clarifying their behaviors.

4. What are the five needs in Maslow's list? Start with the lowest or most basic.

5. Explain the first four needs.

6. What are the known verses as a basis for your faith?

PERSONALITY STRUCTURE:
TAKING APART THE WATCH TO
SEE WHAT MAKES IT TICK
CHAPTER FIVE

<u>QUESTIONS:</u>

1. How a person mentally evaluates an event determines what?

   ____

   ____

   ____

2. Draw a picture of someone that has deep emotional reaction.

3. Draw a picture of someone of worthlessness and sustained by the safety it provides from further failure.

4. What are the elements of personalities?

   ____

   ____

   ____

   ____

   ____

5. What kind of person is this diagram?

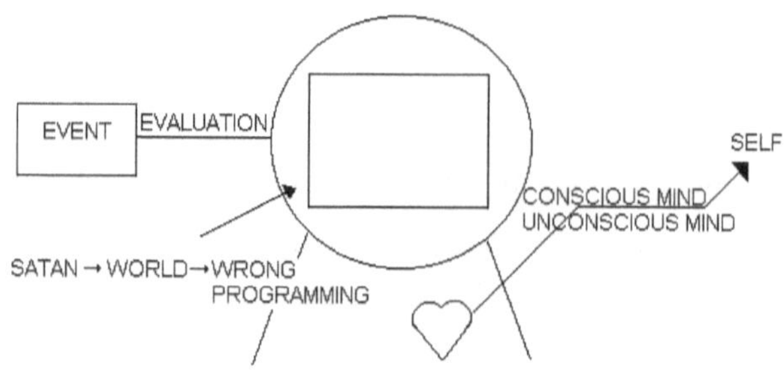

6. What would a Christian whose heart is truly committed to Christ look like?

7. Explain the use of will for the Diagram.

8. What is the last thing that will complete the drawing on human personality?

9. Compare Column A and B according to the Bible and negative emotions.

10. What does transformation depend on?

HOW PROBLEMS DEVELOP I
CHAPTER SIX

QUESTIONS:

1. Why is it that need it is the first concept of the model?

    ____

    ____

2. What is the second concept in the model?

    ____

    ____

3. Draw a sketch to fit question 1 and 2.

4. People develop one broad, guiding area. Write out the examples given.
    I will be significant if:

    ____

    ____

    ____

    (4. continued)
    I will be secure if:

    ____

    ____

    ____

    ____

5. When children latch on to a basic assumption, their motivation acquires direction. A goal is set. "Set a patter to help set a goal"?

6. Explain the two diagrams: Diagram 1 and Diagram 2

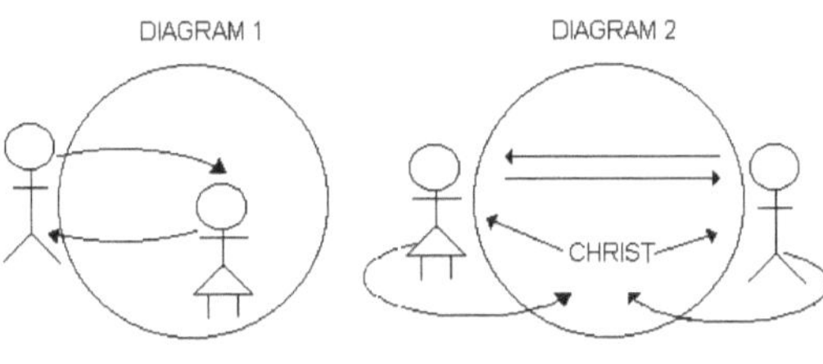

____

____

____

____

7. What did our Lord tell the Samaritan woman about being content?

____

____

8. What two sentences add to the diagram that now reflects how most "well adjusted" people live?

____

____

9. Add death to the diagram. Now show what it looks like."

____

____

HOW PROBLEMS DEVELOP II
CHAPTER SEVEN

<u>QUESTIONS:</u>

1. What are the three categories that frustrated people fall into?

2. Place each word with the right category.
   Resentment, anxiety and guilt.

Category #1

   <u>Category #2</u>

Category #3

3. Draw a diagram that Miller and Dollard has put together. Then explain it.

4. Psychosomatic symptom can be the direct physical result of unhealthy emotional states. True or False?

5. Is it true or false that the behavior: emotional problem of anxiety, resentment and guilt, have direct effects on sexual functioning?

18

WHAT DO YOU TRY TO CHANGE?
CHAPTER EIGHT

<u>QUESTIONS:</u>

1. In order to develop a counseling strategy, we must decide what?

2. Are you trying to change how the client feels? Do we simply try to eliminate his symptoms?

3. Christian counselors believe that a persons welfare depends on what?

4. What is the primary problem with people today?

5. What does transformation depend on?

6. What does it mean to change the goal of a person meaningfully?

7. Draw your goals within the circle, and what does it mean?

8. Now draw your experience with basic anxiety.

____

____

____

____

____

____

9. What factor does therapists try to change and how?

____

____

____

10. When that belief is changed and the client is acting upon his
    new biblical belief, he is on his way to the goal of what?

____

____

____

A SIMPLE MODEL FOR COUNSELING
CHAPTER NINE

<u>QUESTIONS:</u>

1. What is referred to Colossians 1:28, Paul states he "___________ confronts" people in an effort to promote their maturity.

   ____

   ____

2. What did Paul tell the Thessalonians to________________ confront those who were disorderly in their actions. People who were stubbornly resisting their responsibilities.

   ____

   ____

3. What is the Greek word for comfort? What does it mean?

   ____

   ____

4. How many stages are there to counseling?

   ____

   ____

5. Draw a diagram in counseling model form.

COUNSELING IN THE CHRISTIAN COMMUNITY
CHAPTER TEN

QUESTIONS:

1. COMPLETE DIAGRAM ON THE LAST PAGE.

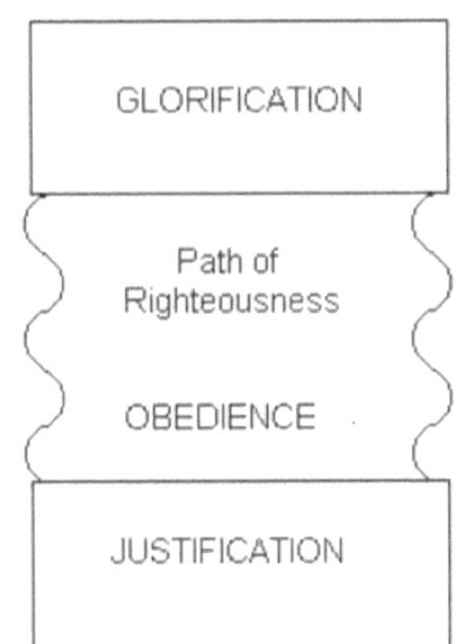

I will be made perfect.
God has predestined it.

In view of my justification and my future glorification, I desire to please the Lord.

I am acceptable to God.
He has declared it.

QUESTIONS:

1. If we are justified, what path should we take to be glorified?

____

____

____

QUESTION:

1. What must a counselor do to help a client to reach the over goal?

____

____

____

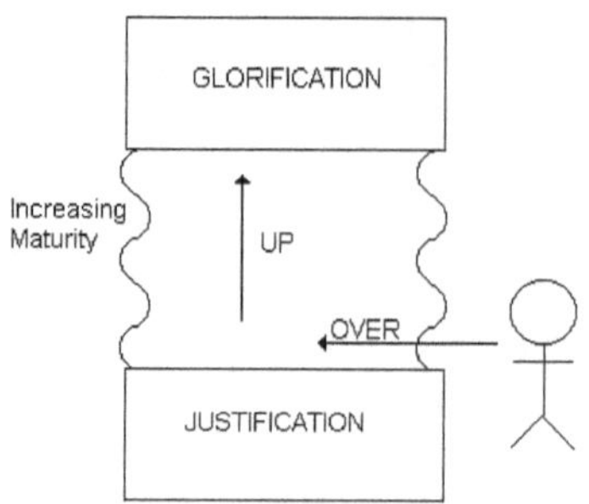

<u>QUESTION:</u>

1. What is the Up Goal?

____

____

____

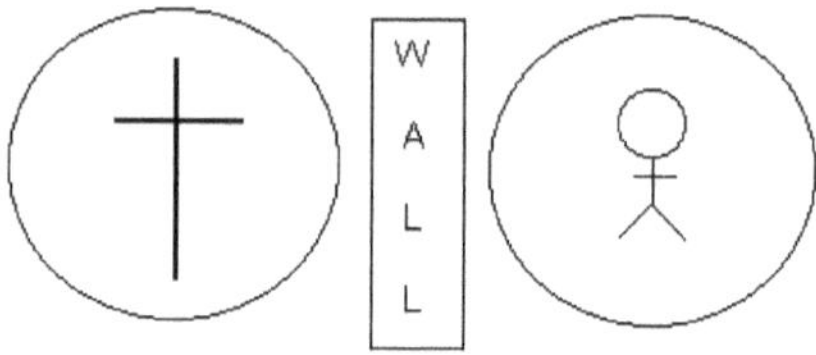

<u>QUESTION:</u>

1. What is the relationship between the two circles?

____

____

____

QUESTION:

1. The weakness of separate but equal is corrected by what?

____

____

____

NOTHING BUTTERY

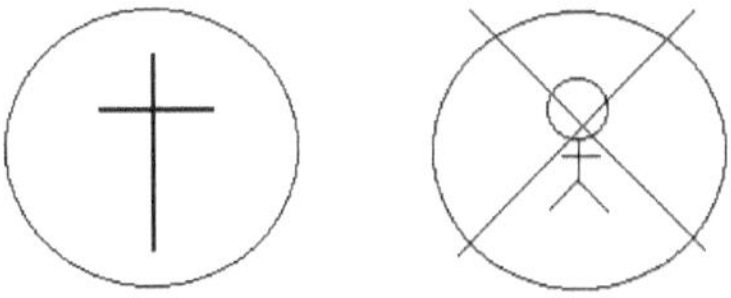

QUESTION:

1. What are basic Butterists tenet?

____

____

____

SPOILING THE EGYPTIAN
Discovered Truth

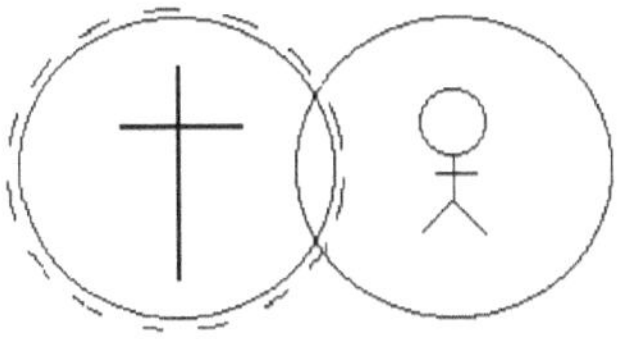

QUESTION:

1. According to this diagram, explain the spoiling of the Egyptian.

____

____

____

____

____

____

____

____

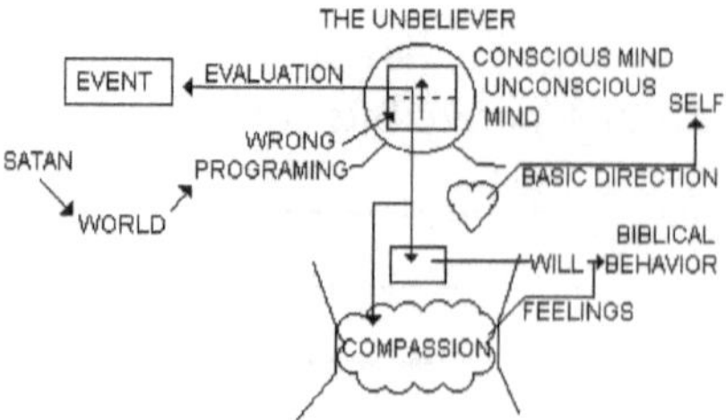

QUESTION:

1.   What kind of sketch is shown on the bottom of the last page?

____

____

____

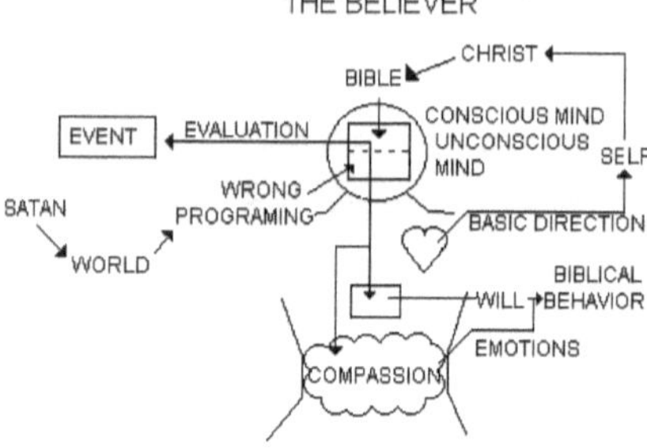

QUESTION:

1.   What kind of sketch is shown above?

____

____

____

____

FILL IN THE BLANKS

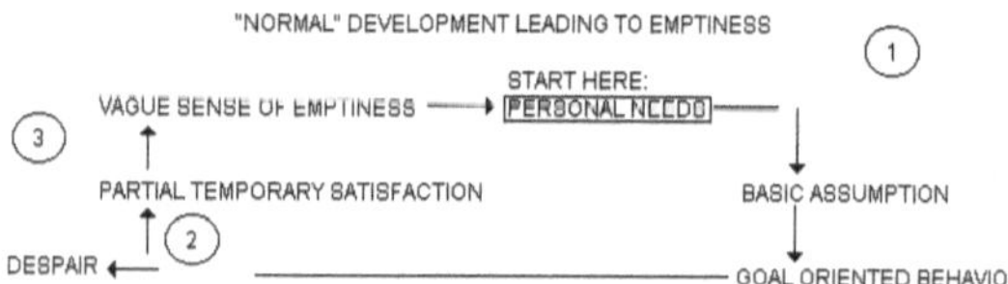

FILL IN THE BLANKS

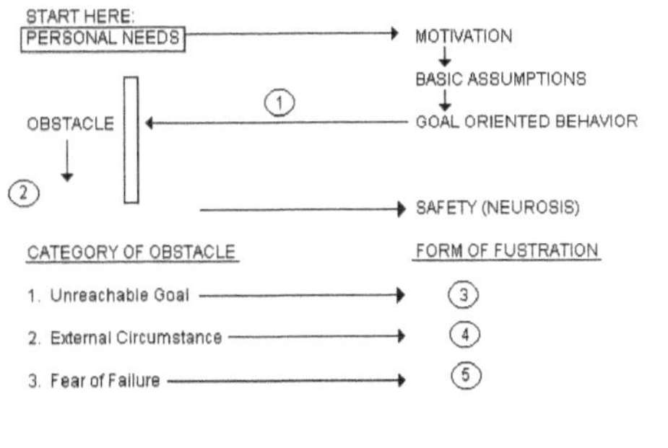

FILL IN THE STAGES BY NUMBERS IN RIGHT ORDER BY ARROWS

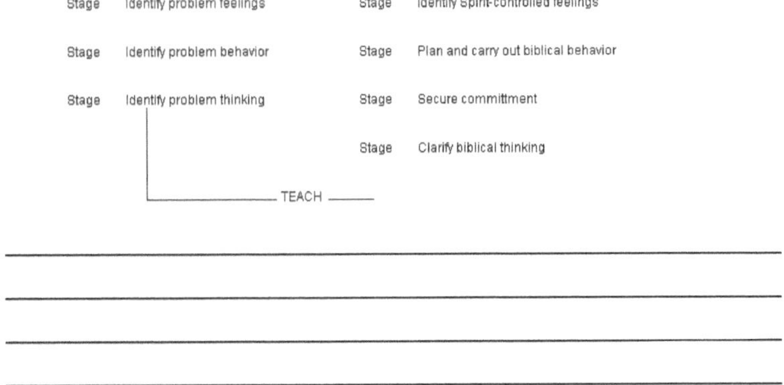

WHAT ARE THE THREE LEVELS OF COUNSELING? FILL IN THE BLANKS.

LEVELS OF COUNSELING
Counseling by:

Level I   Problem Feelings ——————— ENCOURAGEMENT ————→ Biblical Feelings

Level II   Problem Behaviors ——————— EXHORTATION ————→ Biblical Behavior

Level III Problem Thinking ——————— ENLIGHTENMENT ————→ Biblical Thinking

____

____

____

____

PSYCHOLOGICAL PROBLEMS

TEXTBOOK:

HOW TO BE A PEOPLE HELPER
BY GARY R. COLLINS

Approved By: Date: Approved By: Date:

_________________________   _________________________

CHANCELLOR   **VERCHER**

"Study to Show Thyself Approved." 2 Timothy 2:15

PSYCHOLOGICAL PROBLEMS   4 CREDIT HOURS

TEXTBOOK: HOW TO BE A PEOPLE HELPER
AUTHOR: GARY R. COLLINS

STUDENTS WILL BE EXPECTED TO READ EACH CHAPTER AND
DO THE EXERCISES IN THE COURSE OUTLINE BY ANSWERING
ALL THE QUESTIONS AND FOREWARDING THE ANSWERS TO
THE TEACHER FOR GRADING AND TEACHER COMMENTS.

IF ADDITIONAL PAPER IS NEEDED TO COMPLETE THE ANSWERS
PLEASE NOTE THE SUBJECT AND PAGE THE ANSWERS ARE
PERTAINING TO.

THE HEART OR THE PEOPLE
CHAPTER ONE

QUESTIONS:

1. In Psalms 46:1 of the Bible explain how God helps people. Matthew 10:8 explain how God uses people to help others.

   A. ____

   ____

   B. ____

   ____

2. What support does the Bible give for "People helping is everybody's business". 1 John 3:17

   ____

   ____

3. What are the three primary characteristics of being a Disciple?

   ____

   ____

4. What was the famous mandate that Jesus gave to the followers who gathered with him on the Mountain of Galilee?

   ____

   ____

5. Jesus proclaimed that if any person wanted to have eternal life in Heaven and abundant life on Earth, he/she must do what?

   ____

   ____

6. What does Disciple mean?

   ____

   ____

7. What do the three characteristics of a Disciple of Jesus Christ; obedience, love and faithfulness mean?

A. ____

B. ____

C. ____

8. What is the cost of Discipleship?

____

____

9. What are the three relationships we must give up to be a Disciple of Jesus Christ?

A. ____

B. ____

C. ____

10. What are the three responsibilities of Discipleship?

A. ____

B. ____

C. ____

11. What are the three approaches to people helping?

A. ____

B. ____

C. ____

12. The place to begin a Christian approach to counseling, however is with what?

____

____

THE BASIC OF PEOPLE HELPING
CHAPTER TWO

<u>QUESTIONS:</u>

1. What is Discipleship counseling?
2. What are the three basic functions on Christian people helping?
   A. ____
   B. ____
   C. ____

3. What are the six people helper principles?
   A. ____
   B. ____
   C. ____
   D. ____
   E. ____
   F. ____

4. What kind of relationship can develop for a person who seeks to build with Jesus Christ, describe in one word.
5. What evidence suggests that effective helpers succeed?
   A. ____
   B. ____
   C. ____

6. What do empathy, warmth and genuineness mean?
   A. Empathy____
   B. Warmth____

   ____

   ____

   C. Genuineness______________________________________

   ____

   ____

7. According to Table 2-1 fill in the blank? What does each one have in common?

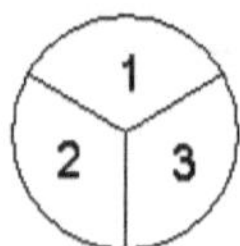

1.____

2. ____

3. ____

____

____

THE TECHNIQUES OF PEOPLE HELPING
CHAPTER 3

<u>QUESTIONS:</u>

1. List the Basic helping skills?

    ____

2. What are the four basic behaviors Ivey listed on attending?

    1.____
    2.____
    3.____
    4.____

3. What are the twelve guidelines for effective listening?

    1.____
    2.____
    3.____
    4.____
    5.____
    6.____
    7.____
    8.____
    9.____
    10.____
    11.____
    12.____

4. What approaches can be used for leading the helpless?

    1.____
    2.____
    3.____
    4.____
    5.____
    6.____

5. What are the influencing skills?

    a. ____

    b. ____

    c. ____

    d. ____

    e. ____

    f. ____

    g. ____

6. What are the five steps in disciplining process? (according to the bible.)

    a. ____

    b. ____

    c. ____

    d. ____

    e. ____

7. What did Jesus teach about helping people, according to what books that are listed?

    ____

    ____

8. Does James 1:19 emphasize the importance of listening? What does it say?

    ____

    ____

9. How should we comfort others? According to Matthew 7:1 and Galatians' 6:1.

    ____

    ____

THE DIRECTION OF PEOPLE HELPING
CHAPTER FOUR

<u>QUESTIONS:</u>

1. Like Jesus, the helper today must be willing to go where the helpless are.

    [] True   [] False

2. What are the six steps in people helping?

    A. ____
    B. ____
    C. ____
    D. ____
    E. ____
    F. ____

3. Explain all steps in 1 – 6.

    1. ____
    2. ____
    3. ____
    4. ____
    5. ____
    6. ____

4. Complete the table that is drawn.

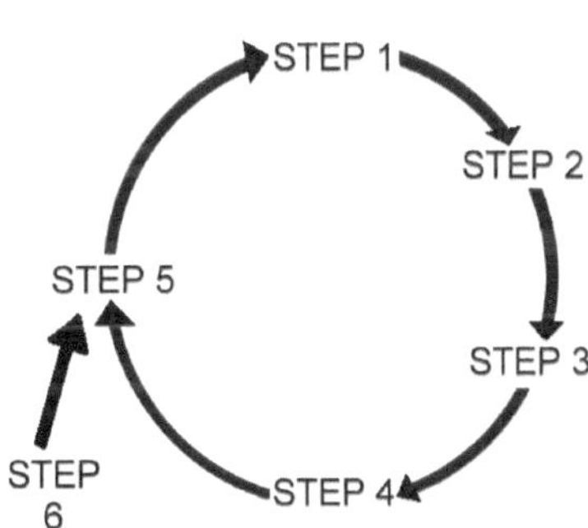

A. 1. ____
    2. ____
    3. ____
    4. ____
    5. ____
    6. ____

PARAPROFESSIONAL PEOPLE HELPING
CHAPTER FIVE

<u>QUESTIONS:</u>

1. If you had a problem and needed help, to whom would you go to and why?

   ____

   ____

2. Does peer counseling work?   [] Yes   [] No
3. Why are peer helpers effective?

   ____

   ____

4. Is counseling a special gift?

   ____

   ____

5. Should every Christian be a people helper?

   ____

   ____

6. What is the Greek word for exhortation and what does it mean?

   ____

   ____

7. What are the eight characteristics for selecting people helpers?

   a. ____

   b. ____

   c. ____

   d. ____

   e. ____

   f. ____

   g. ____

   h. ____

STRESS AND PEOPLE HELPING
CHAPTER SIX

<u>QUESTIONS:</u>

1. What are the two categories that stress is divided into? Explain.

   ____

   ____

2. Draw a diagram that will enable us to understand the meaning of stress more clearly.

   ____

   ____

3. List the spiritual Stress.
   A.____
   B.____
   C.____
   D.____
   E.____
   F.____

4. What are the spiritual symptoms of stress?
   A.____
   B.____
   C.____
   D.____

5. What are the ways that we may use to help people handle stress?

A. ____

B. ____

C. ____

D. ____

E. ____

F. ____

6. These verses speak about what? Romans 1:11-12, 1 Thess. 4:18, 1 Thess. 5:11, Heb. 3:13 and Heb 10:24-25

____

____

7. Who was one of the most admired individuals in the New Testament? From where and what did they call him and what does it mean?

____

____

8. Who did Barnabus encourage?

____

____

9. How did the letter begin?

____

____

10. What did Paul write?

____

____

11. Who did Paul write a positive letter to?

____

____

12. How did Paul encourage Timothy?

____

____

13. Throughout Paul's letter, he gives helpful hints, what are they?
    A.____
    B.____

14. How can someone be a people helper?
    A.____

    ____

    B.____

    ____

HELPING IN CRISIS
CHAPTER SEVEN

<u>QUESTIONS:</u>

1. What two broad categories can crisis be divided into?
   A. ____
   B. ____

2. There are two ways in helping people in a time of crisis, what are they?

   ____

   ____

3. In the midst of crisis, most people are confused and uncertain of what to do,
   [] True   [] False

4. What approach can be used for helping a person in crisis?
   A. ____
   B. ____
   C. ____
   D. ____
   E. ____

5. Was Jesus ever a crisis counselor? Explain according to John 11.

   ____

   ____

6. How did God use crisis?
   A. ____
   B. ____

HELPING WHEN PEOPLE ARE DESPARATE
CHAPTER EIGHT

<u>QUESTIONS:</u>

1. How many suicides does the Bible record?

   ____

   ____

2. What two are best known?

   ____

   ____

3. What five types of evaluating suicide potential must the helper keep in mind?
   A. ____
   B. ____
   C. ____
   D. ____
   E. ____

4. Is suicide common with religious people?
   [] Yes   [] No

5. In suicide preventing, somebody suggested that we as people helper need what?

   ____

   ____

6. Is the scripture Exodus 18 a good place for referrals of preventing suicide?
   [] Yes   [] No

HELPING ON THE PHONE
CHAPTER NINE

<u>QUESTIONS:</u>

1. Is telephone help less threatening? Explain.

    ____

    ____

2. Why do helpless people feel more comfortable talking on the phone from their own home?

    ____

    ____

3. Can telephone help be anonymous and available? [] Yes [] No
4. When is telephone counseling helpful?

    ____

    ____

5. What are the limitations of telephone helping?

    ____

    ____

6. What are the unique features in telephone counseling that is no different from any other kind of people helping?
    A. ____
    B. ____
    C. ____
    D. ____
    E. ____

7. Can and should the gospel be presented over the phone?
    [] Yes   [] No

HELPING IN THE CHURCH
CHAPTER TEN

<u>QUESTIONS:</u>

1. Doing Jesus ministry here on Earth his main concern was about what? And what chapter of the Bible?

2. In what book of the New Testament deals with one fifth of all verses of healing?

3. When Jesus was here on Earth and returned to Heaven, following the resurrection, is it true his physical body disappeared from Earth? But he left another body to carry on his work: Is this statement True or False? Explain.

4. What is the Biblical view of the Church?

5. Where do spiritual gifts come from?

6. What are the two purposes that Gifts of the Holy Spirit have?
   1.

   2.

7. What does spiritual gift have to do with being an authentic people helper?

____

____

____

8. The body of Christ exists for a number of purposes, what are they?
    A. ____
    B. ____
    C. ____

9. The New Testament uses the Greek word, Koionia to describe this kind of fellowship, Christian fellowship is the continual expressions of what?

____

____

10. When Jesus was asked how a person could be great his reply was what?

____

____

11. Being a Christian, you should be submissive to one another and to serve one another, is this a self-centered or other-centered way of living?

____

____

HELPING BY PREVENTION
CHAPTER ELEVEN

<u>QUESITONS:</u>

1. What are the three aims of preventive helping?
   A. ____
   B. ____
   C. ____

2. Another name for the three aims are called?
   A. ____
   B. ____
   C. ____

3. In the Bible, four words described Jesus as a person of what?
   A. ____
   B. ____
   C. ____
   D. ____

4. What scripture gives a superb example of preventive counseling techniques that Jesus used?

5. What are Jesus methods for preventing future problems?
   A. ____
   B. ____
   C. ____
   D. ____
   E. ____
   F. ____
   G. ____

6. What are the attitudes on part of the helper, Christians should recognize?
   A. ____

B. ____

C. ____

D. ____

E. ____

F. ____

7. What is the guideline that Jesus provided to help us achieve here knowing living in this world it would be difficult?

A. ____

B. ____

C. ____

D. ____

E. ____

HELPING YOURSELF
CHAPTER TWELVE

QUESTIONS:

1. What are the three levels of self examination that are important to yourself?
    1. _____________________________________
    2. _____________________________________
    3. _____________________________________

2. Why is self-image important?

3. What is the unpopular word that describes human rebellion? Where is it found in your Bible?

4. An immature person who have trouble understanding the Bible is called what?

5. To grow as a Christian we need to do what?

6. Who has a problem of working? He said he has a "Throne in the flesh" that kept him worried. What did he do about it?

BASIC PRINCIPLES FOR COUNSELING AFRICAN AMERICANS

TEXTBOOK:

BIBLICAL COUNSELING WITH AFRICAN AMERICANS
BY CLARENCE WALKER

Approved By: Date: Approved By: Date:

CHANCELLOR   *VERCHER*

"Study to Show Thyself Approved." 2 Timothy 2:15

BASIC PRINCIPLES OF COUNSELING   4 CREDIT HOURS

TEXTBOOK: BIBLICAL COUNSELING WITH AFRICAN AMERICANS
AUTHOR: CLARENCE WALKER

THE PURPOSE OF THIS COURSE IS TO INTRODUCE THE
STUDENT TO THE BASIC PRINCIPLE OF COUNSELING THROUGH
EXAMINING A BALANCE VIEW OF PEOPLE, PROBLEMS AND
SOLUTIONS.

STUDENTS WILL BE EXPECTED TO READ EACH CHAPTER AND
DO THE EXERCISES IN THE COURSE OUTLINE BY ANSWERING
ALL THE QUESTIONS AND FOREWARDING THE ANSWERS TO
THE TEACHER FOR GRADING AND TEACHER COMMENTS.

IF ADDITIONAL PAPER IS NEEDED TO COMPLETE THE ANSWERS
PLEASE NOTE THE SUBJECT AND PAGE THE ANSWERS ARE
PERTAINING TO.

INTRODUCTION

<u>QUESTIONS:</u>

1. The biblical counseling with African Americans is a book based upon what?

   ____

   ____

   ____

2. What is the purpose of this book?

   ____

   ____

   ____

3. What are the three integrated components of biblical counseling with black counselors?

   ____

   ____

   ____

4. What are the three parts that biblical counseling with African Americans are divided into?

   ____

   ____

   ____

5. What did the Holy Spirit enable Philip to do?

   ____

   ____

   ____

"A MAN OF ETHIOPIA" (ACTS 8:27)
CHAPTER ONE

QUESTIONS:

1. What was the first challenges faced by Philip in Acts 8:27?

    ____

    ____

2. If counselors are to experience a successful chariot ride through the course of counseling, it is important that they do what?

    ____

    ____

WEST AFRICAN FAMILIAL STRUCTURS

1. What are the several things that we can learn about kinship as a counselor from West Africans history?

    ____

    ____

    ____

    ____

2. To get a better understanding about black families, it is important to know what two sources form their familial identity. What are they?

    ____

    ____

BLACK SELF-CONCEPT DEVELOPMENT

1. What is the issue of black self-concept and its shape by three cultural sources?

    ____

    ____

2. What does James Dobson say about blacks suffering from low self-esteem?

    ____

    ____

3. What do we read in Psalm 139:14?

    ____

    ____

4. What must Christian counselors enable and encourage African Americans?

    ____

    ____

    ____

    ____

BLACK COUNSELORS AND WHITE COUNSELORS

1. What are the differences between black counselors and white counselors?

    ____

    ____

2. What was the question the prophet asked in Jeremiah 13:23, and what was the answer?

    ____

    ____

GENDER ISSUES – "A MAN OF ETHIOPIA" (ACTS 8:27)
CHAPTER TWO

QUESTIONS:

1. When Philip arose and went to join the man of Ethiopia what was he up against?

____

____

2. For black men, what has been a sensitive factor for them in America?

____

____

BLACK MASCULINITY

1. What is read in Ephesians 5:23?

____

____

BLACK MALE AND FEMALE INTERACTIVE DYNAMICS

1. Is there no live in black marriages or do these couples define love differently than whites?

____

____

2. Why does Jill Nelson claim black men fear love?

____

____

____

SEXUAL ISSUES – "A EUNUCH" (ACTS 8:27)
CHAPTER THREE

QUESTIONS:

1. What does it mean to be a eunuch and to be castrated?

   ____

   ____

SEXUALITY, SEXUAL ORIENTATIONS AND BLACKS COUNSELESS

1. As a Christian, is it normal to have sexual feelings, Yes or No? Explain.

   ____

   ____

2. What does ISD mean?

   ____

   ____

3. What is the most common disruption in black males marriages?

   ____

   ____

4. Why do single women seek married men?

   ____

   ____

5. Should a hypersexual person seek a psychiatrist? And should a Christian counselor refer them to one? Yes or No?

   ____

   ____

1. Is it true that blacks have been the victims of stereotypes with respect to their sexuality? True or False.

    ____

    ____

2. What are the roles that black men and black women have been portraying? Explain.

    ____

    ____

3. Is it true that whites are threatened by blacks sexual powers? True or False.

    ____

    ____

THE CHRISTIAN VIEW OF SEX

1. Why should Christians possess the most accurate understanding of sex?

    ____

    ____

2. What are the four biblical postulates understanding of sex that Herbert Miles argues?

    ____

    ____

    ____

    ____

3. What does the bible say about the understanding of sex? Referred to answers 1 – 4?

    ____

    ____

POWER ISSUES – "OF GREAT AUTHORITY" (ACTS 8:27)
CHAPTER FOUR

<u>QUESTIONS:</u>

1. What was the fourth issue faced by Philip?

   ____

   ____

2. Who had even more than the black man?

   ____

   ____

POWERLESSNESS AND THE BLACK MALE

1. In George Gilder's book what is the greatest enemy to black progress in America?

   ____

   ____

2. Black female is in some ways, more powerless than the male? True or False.

   ____

   ____

POWERLESSNESS AND THE BLACK FEMALE

1. We know that men are supposed to be head of the house. Explain the bind a born again Christian wife can get into?

   ____

   ____

1. What do Christian counselors need to do in the face of powerlessness?

    ____

    ____

2. What is probably the second leading cause of marital conflict among black couples?

    ____

    ____

SOCIO-ECONOMIC ISSUES
CHAPTER FIVE

<u>QUESTIONS:</u>

1. Who was responsible for the queen's money?

   ____

   ____

2. What issue does Christian counselors face when dealing with black counselors?

   ____

   ____

SOCIO-ECONOMICS AND BLACK FAMILY STRUCTURE

1. What is often a response to economic pressure of black families?

   ____

   ____

SOCIO-ECONOMICS AND MARITAL SATISFACTION

1. Explain the relationship between marital satisfaction and economics for black couples. There are three each.

   ____

   ____

   ____

   ____

   ____

   ____

   ____

   ____

   ____

ENVIRONMENTAL ISSUES
CHAPTER SIX

<u>QUESTIONS:</u>

1. What are the two kinds of environment dimensions that require attention in the black counselees?

____

____

HOME ENVIRONMENT INFLUENCES

1. Home environment is more than a physical structure with dimensions. It has what?

____

____

2. What important roles does home environment play?

____

____

COMMUNITY ENVIRONMENTAL INFLUENCES

1. Christian counselors must help black counselees break this cycle of hopelessness by doing what?

____

____

2. Do you agree or disagree with the power that a black man can have and changes he can make with a newfound hope in Christ?

____

____

DIRECTIVE ENGAGING
CHAPTER SEVEN

QUESTIONS:

1. Philip's first activities were described as what? And what does it mean?

   ____

   ____

2. Who directed Philip to pursue the mission with the eunuch?

   ____

   ____

GOD'S LEADING IN ENGAGING

1. What reasons are God's leading imperatives in the engaging process?

   ____

   ____

   ____

   ____

2. What are the two necessary tasks in the directive engaging process?

   ____

   ____

DIFFICULTIES ENGAGING BLACK COUNSELEES

1. The only difficulties blacks may have entering into a session, particularly if the counselors are white would be what?

   ____

   ____

1. Can white therapists effectively counsel blacks? Yes or No. Explain.

   ____

   ____

2. What are the few rules white Christian counselors should follow? And why?

   ____

   ____

   ____

   ____

   ____

   ____

   ____

   ____

   ____

   Finally, what must Christian counselors look for in black behavior?

   ____

   ____

   ____

   ____

3. When does the are of engaging begin?

   ____

   ____

4. Explain engagement.

   ____

   ____

   ____

   ____

5. Bruce Narramore gives an example of the air of engaging. What is it? What is the first step?

____

____

____

____

EFFECTIVE JOINING
CHAPTER EIGHT

QUESTIONS:

1. The principle of effective joining is reflected in what book of the Bible?

2. What instructed Philip to join himself to the Ethiopians chariot?

RESPECTING THE ETHIOPIAN'S CHARIOT

1. Explain the symbol of the Ethiopian's chariot. What does it represent?

2. When is the right moment for joining to happen?

METHODS OF JOINING

1. According to the Bible, explain the method of humor.

2. How was Philip able to enter the chariot?

3. What is active listening?

ACTIVE LISTENING
CHAPTER NINE

<u>QUESTIONS:</u>

1. According to the Bible active listening is emphasized in what role?

   ____

   ____

LISTENING AS A MEANS OF ASSESSING AND GATHERING DATA

1. What book can you find this verse: "Out of the abundance of the heart the mouth speaketh."

   ____

   ____

2. Important details of a problem and counselor's folly are described in?

   ____

   ____

LISTENING FOR AFFECT AND FEELING

1. What must we look for in active listening?

   ____

   ____

2. Listening for feelings involves the use of one's spiritual gut and more than one's ears; one must listen for the feeling behind the feelings. True or False?

   ____

   ____

1. What does empathy mean?

    ____

    ____

LISTENING FOR MEANING AND USE OF LANGUAGE

1. Language is a two-edged sword. True or False?

    ____

    ____

2. Why is it that low-income blacks may have problems communicating?

    ____

    ____

EXPLORATIVE QUESTIONING
CHAPTER TEN

<u>QUESTIONS:</u>

1. Is the question in Acts 8:30 an explorative question Yes or No?

   ____

   ____

2. What are precautions to take when using explorative query with black counselees?

   ____

   ____

USE OF QUESTIONS

1. What several reasons may questions be used?

   ____

   ____

   ____

   ____

2. What does good explorative questioning involve?

   ____

   ____

3. How must good explorative questions be asked?

   ____

   ____

CORRELATIVE BEGINNING
CHAPTER ELEVEN

<u>QUESTIONS:</u>

1. What are the two steps in correlative beginning?

   ____

   ____

2. What are other signs of counselees getting stuck and what must counselors do to be alert to redundant behavioral, intrapsychic and systemic patterns that indicate counselees are stuck?

   ____

   ____

   ____

   ____

3. What happens if counselors do not recognize this phenomenon?

   ____

   ____

SELECTING INTERVENTIVE STARTING POINTS

1. What is the first step in the process for those black counselees?

   ____

   ____

INTREGRATIVE WITNESSING
CHAPTER TWELVE

<u>QUESTIONS:</u>

1. What is the work preached in the New Testament Greek is and what does it mean?

____

____

FIVE USES OF THE GOSPEL

1. What are the five uses of the Gospel?

____

____

____

____

____

____

DEALING WITH THE THREE KINDS OF SINNERS

1. What are the three kinds of sinners discussed in Romans 1-3?

____

____

2. What does all three sinners have in common?

____

____

OBJECTIVE PROCEEDING
CHAPTER THIRTEEN

<u>QUESTIONS:</u>

1. What goals must counselees and counselors agree on?

   ____

   ____

THE GOALS OF BIBLICAL COUNSELING

1. What are the three stages Collins put counseling goals and objectives in context?

   ____

   ____

   ____

   ____

   ____

   ____

GOAL SETTING AS AN EMPOWERING TOOL

1. Counselors use goal setting in a number of ways to empower counselees, what are they?

   ____

   ____

   ____

   ____

   ____

EFFECTIVE COUNSELING
CHAPTER FOURTEEN

<u>QUESTIONS:</u>

1. When is it at the point the counselor's wisdom, experience, knowledge and expertise are summoned?

    ____

    ____

2. What does Biblical counseling deal with?

    ____

    ____

ROLES FOR CHRISTIAN COUNSELORS

1. Whatever roles counselors utilize must be done in what context?

    ____

    ____

LEVELS OF BIBLICAL COUNSELING

1. What are the three levels of Christian counseling?

    ____

    ____

2. At all three levels, Biblical counselors must be aware of what?

    ____

    ____

COOPERATIVE INVOLVING
CHAPTER FIFTEEN

<u>QUESTIONS:</u>

1. What is cooperative involving?

____

____

____

____

COUNSELEE BLOCKS TO COOPERATIVE INVOLVING

1. What are the two forms of counselee blocks to cooperative involving?

____

____

____

COUNSELOR BLOCKS TO COOPERATIVE INVOLVING

1. Counselors do not work hard enough to fulfill the needs of counselees when needed. True or False?

____

____

____

POSITIVE TERMINATING
CHAPTER SIXTEEN

<u>QUESTIONS:</u>

1. After Philip finished baptizing the eunuch, what kind of remarkable divine experience did they have?

2. Termination of therapy is more than just saying good-bye; what is it?

THE ROLE OF THE HOLY SPIRIT IN TERMINATION

1. Philip's relationship with the Ethiopian was literally terminated by what?

2. In order to prepare counselees for termination, counselors must do what?

QUESTIONS:

1. What are the two critical factors that influence black marriages?
2. Marital problems are a deviation of what book?

3. Couples with a strong religious orientation then to do what in therapy?

BIBLICAL MARITAL COUNSELING WITH BLACK COUPLES

1. Why do most couples go to counseling?

2. What problems do black women have?

3. What is a critical issue in bringing black couples to therapy?

BIBLICAL THERAPEUTIC INTERVENTIONS

1. What are the five approaches for use with black couples?

2. What are the several communication styles with black Christian couples?

____

____

BIBLICAL INDIVIDUAL THERAPY

1. When doing individual therapy, what three approaches are effective with African American counselees?

____

____

CONCLUSION

1. What was the aim of this section?

____

____

2. Clarence Walker saw seven challenges that Philip face as a Christian counselor. What were they?

_______________   _______________

_______________   _______________

_______________   _______________

_______________   _______________

_______________   _______________

3. Clarence Walker recognized the interactions between Philip and the Ethiopian; that was what?

____

____

____

____

____

____

____

CHRISTIAN COUNSELING

TEXTBOOK:
HOW TO HELP PEOPLE CHANGE
BY JAY E. ADAMS

Approved By: Date: Approved By: Date:

CHANCELLOR   **_VERCHER_**

"Study to Show Thyself Approved." 2 Timothy 2:15

CHRISTIAN COUNSELING   ___ CREDIT HOURS

TEXTBOOK: HOW TO HELP PEOPLE CHANGE
AUTHOR: JAY E. ADAMS

THE PURPOSE OF THIS COURSE IS TO PROVIDE THE STUDENT
WITH PARTICULAR ASPECTS OF COUNSELING, TO ELUCIDATE
THE PROCESS OF COUNSELING AND TO AID THE COUNSELOR
OR STUDENT WITH TECHNIQUES THAT WILL HELP PEOPLE
CHANGE.

STUDENTS WILL BE EXPECTED TO READ EACH CHAPTER AND
DO THE EXERCISES IN THE COURSE OUTLINE BY ANSWERING
ALL THE QUESTIONS AND FOREWARDING THE ANSWERS TO
THE TEACHER FOR GRADING AND TEACHER COMMENTS.

IF ADDITIONAL PAPER IS NEEDED TO COMPLETE THE ANSWERS
PLEASE NOTE THE SUBJECT AND PAGE THE ANSWERS ARE
PERTAINING TO.

THE NEED OF INNER CHANGE
CHAPTER ONE

<u>QUESTIONS:</u>

1. When someone finds it difficult to get along with others, most people agree something has got to change.
   [   ] True   [   ] False

2. Explain what is meant by "human relationships are a three-way, not two-way affairs."

   ____

   ____

3. Even though the Pharisee was a good man and fairly with himself, Jesus saw it differently. What did Jesus state to him?

   ____

   ____

4. How many kinds of competing "Good" are there in this world?

   ____

   ____

5. According to Matthew 7:6, what is meant by "restraining evil is not the same as promoting good"?

   ____

   ____

6. God had appointed Christian counselors as guides to a change that is directed towards Godliness, what are the changes?

   a.____

   b. ____

   c. ____

THE FOUR STEP BIBLICAL PROCESS
CHAPTER TWO

<u>QUESTIONS:</u>

1. What was the purpose of Paul's writing to 2 Timothy 3:14-17?

   ____

   ____

2. What was written to Timothy in Paul's last letter to him?

   ____

   ____

3. What are the two characteristics of scripture that 2 Timothy reads in verses 14-17?

   a.____

   ____

   b.____

   ____

4. What two uses of scripture represent two stages in ministering to people?

   a.____

   b.____

5. The two stages of ministering to people are called what?

   a.____

   b.____

6. What are the four steps to edification?

   a._______________________   b._______________________

   c._______________________   d._______________________

THE CHANGE PRODUCING CHARACTER OF THE SCRIPTURE
CHAPTER THREE

QUESTIONS:

1. Paul gives five scriptural credentials, what are they?

   a.____

   b.____

   c.____

   d.____

   e.____

2. From the New Testament, what are the two words that "Holy" are translated?

   a.____

   b.____

3. What two words are used to speak of the temple and saved place?

   ____

   ____

4. When Paul wrote of the ability of the scriptures to make a person wise about salvation in Christ Jesus, what was he literally saying?

   ____

   ____

5. What was the purpose of the spirit moving when John wrote his gospel?

   ____

   ____

6. What does John's gospel demonstrate?

   ____

   ____

7. What is meant by the word inspired?

____

____

8. Can the writers inspire us?   [   ] Yes [   ] No
9. Can we be inspired by what the writers have written?
    [   ] Yes [   ] No

10. Is there a difference between inspired writers and inspired
    writing? [   ] Yes [   ] No
11. What does the original Greek word say about inspired?

____

____

12. What does inspired mean?

____

____

13. Is the Bible profitable? [   ] Yes [   ] No
14. What is the English word for profitable?

____

____

15. How can the Bible be neglected?

____

____

16. God's word must be ministered to his people in such a way that
    their lives must do what?

____

____

____

____

THE SUFFICIENCY OF SCRIPTURE
CHAPTER FOUR

<u>QUESTIONS:</u>

1. What are the three small verses Paul emphasized on the sufficiency of scriptures?

    a._______________________________

    b. ______________________________

    c. ______________________________

2. What does the word translated adequate mean?

    ____

3. What is the second term and what does it mean?

    ____

4. Is there any relationship between psychology and Christian counseling that can be fruitful? [   ] Yes [   ] No

5. Is there any necessary relationship between psychology and Christian counseling? [   ] Yes [   ] No

6. In verse 17 Paul says the same thing three different ways in order to make his point. What did he say?

    a._______________________________

    b. ______________________________

    c. ______________________________

7. Is there a relationship between Christian and legitimate psychology?

    ____

8. There are two commandments that are the subject matter of all counseling that the Bible hangs on to. What are they?

    ____

THE HUMAN AND DIVINE ROLES IN CHANGE
CHAPTER FIVE

<u>QUESTIONS:</u>

1. What two unbiblical extremes must Christian counselors avoid?

   a.____

   b. ____

2. It is equally unbiblical for counselors to do nothing while waiting for God to do everything. [   ] True [   ] False

3. What are the four elements that change in the process of counseling that must be interrelated?

   a.________________________ b.________________________

   c.________________________ d. ________________________

4. What is the production of the bible that the spirit produced through divinely aided humans?

   ____

   ____

5. How does the Holy Spirit operate?

   ____

   ____

6. What are the four functions of scripture said to be performed also by the Holy Spirit?

   a.____

   b. ____

   c. ____

   d. ____

7. In each of the four functions, how does the Holy Spirit work?

   ____

   ____

8. Counselors must neither add to nor subtract from God's words, "but offer those needing help, the whole counsel of God."
[   ] True [   ] False

9. What does the Greek word Spoudazo mean? (2 Timothy 2:15)

____

____

10. According to 1 Kings 17:24, a man of God is or who has what?

____

____

11. What is Timothy rightly called and why?

____

____

THE IMPORTANCE OF TEACHING
CHAPTER SIX

<u>QUESTIONS:</u>

1. Name the first of the four consideration steps of the process of change in the order set fourth by Paul?

   ____

   ____

2. How does Jesus describe John's gospel?

   ____

   ____

3. What did Jesus say in Matthew 28:20 about teaching?

   ____

   ____

4. Once a disciple is fully trained he will be like whom?

   ____

   ____

5. Will teachers receive a stricter judgment because they are men from God?

   ____

   ____

TEACHING GOD'S STANDARDS
CHAPTER SEVEN

<u>QUESTIONS:</u>

1. What should a counselor look like?

2. Give detail of Jesus life from the ten commencements.

3. Paul offers hope that is sure, based on what?

4. Paul writes of what kind of hope?

5. According to Paul, explain how the Holy Spirit generate this hope in the heart of those that believe.

6. Where does hope come from?

7. Where doe the Holy Spirit come from?

8. When you instruct a person in God's will, but they do not obey they must do what?

____

____

9. What is the Spirit who enlighten?

____

____

10. What must both the counselor and counselee ask God for in order to make a change?

____

____

11. In what way must the Bible be used in counseling?

TEACHING BIBLICAL PRINCIPLES
CHAPTER EIGHT

<u>QUESITONS:</u>

1. How do you help a counselee become dependent on God and his word, rather than on human counselors?

    ____

    ____

2. How do you prepare someone for the long hall?

    ____

    ____

3. How critical and effective is the long hall to counseling?
    a.____
    b. ____

4. What was the doctrine of radical amputation Jesus taught frequently?

    ____

    ____

5. What was the purpose for such amputation? It was a way of what?
    a.____
    b. ____

6. What were Jesus' strong words about being thrown in Gehenna?

    ____

    ____

7. What kind of authority do Christian counselors have?

    ____

    ____

8. Explain the works of the Christian counselor?

   ____

   ____

9. What one thing is the Christian counselor to be an expert in?

   ____

   ____

10. Explain the meaning of each word.
    Diakonia Tou Logou_____________________________

    ____

    Diakonos____

    ____

    Etymology_______________________________________

    ____

    Dominie____

    ____

11. What does nouthetic counselor mean and come from?

    ____

    ____

12. What does "temptation" mean according to the King James
    Version?
    [   ] Trial or [   ] Test

TEACHING IN THE MILIEU
CHAPTER NINE

<u>QUESTIONS:</u>

1. What great advantage does a counselor have over the preacher?

    ____

    ____

2. What does teaching in the milieu mean?

    ____

    ____

3. There are two major benefits that arise when teaching in the milieu, what are they?

    a.____

    b. ____

4. Can counselors benefit from the presence of learning in the milieu? [   ] Yes [   ] No

5. Did God use the milieu method of teaching? Is this the method he wants us as counselors to use? [   ] Yes [   ] No

6. What is the 1 Corinthians all about?

    ____

    ____

7. When preaching of counseling they must learn to teach people in what kind of manner?

    ____

    ____

8. Why is homework vitally important to give by the counselor?

    a.____

    b. ____

    c. ____

HOW TO TEACH
CHAPTER TEN

<u>QUESTIONS:</u>

1. Personal involvement. Explain the keys to knowing how to communicate truth in the counseling context.

    ____

    ____

2. What does Paul mean by carrying others burdens?

    ____

    ____

3. Why is involvement important in teaching?

    ____

    ____

4. According to Paul, what does love require us to do?

    ____

    ____

5. What is the problem with the double-minded man?

    ____

    ____

6. Enthusiasm – What is mean by "I am going to vomit you out of my mouth" ? (Revelations 3:15-16)

    ____

    ____

7. Color and vividness – What are the four uses of examples, incidences or illustrations in counseling?

    a._____________________   b._____________________

    c._____________________   d._____________________

8. What are some of the graphic language that Jesus taught that sticks in our minds?

   a.____

   b. ____

   c. ____

   d. ____

   e. ____

   f. ____

   g. ____

THE ROLE OF CONVICTION IN COUNSELING
CHAPTER ELEVEN

QUESTIONS:

1. Why is conviction a sacred step in the process of change?

    ____

    ____

2. What does the Bible require that counselors learn?

    ____

    ____

3. Does the Holy Spirit Convict? [   ] Yes [   ] No
4. Why is conviction so important?

    ____

    ____

5. Why does God convict us and go through the trouble of arguing the case of our wrong?

    ____

    ____

6. How does God feel about fellowship?

    ____

    ____

WHAT IS CONVICTION?
CHAPTER TWELVE

<u>QUESTIONS:</u>

1. What three ways is the word conviction commonly used?
   a.____
   b. ____
   c. ____

2. What can we learn from these gracious words? - "To these commands he then added to assurance, I convict and discipline those about whom I care."

   ____

   ____

3. What does the verb in Verse 19 philco mean?

   ____

   ____

4. What is the conviction of which Jesus spoke and what effect should it have had?

   ____

   ____

5. What are the two definitions that trench's gives?
   a.____
   b. ____

6. What does the word Holy Spirit called and what is the use for it?

   ____

   ____

7. What does John 14:26 say about the Holy Spirit?

   ____

   ____

CONVICTION AND DATA GATHERING
CHAPTER THIRTEEN

<u>QUESTIONS:</u>

1. Why is data gathering essential to counseling a counselee?

   ____

   ____

2. What is the data you must gather?

   a.____

   b. ____

   c. ____

3. 1 John 3:4 Explain what lawbreakers do, according to the chapter?

   ____

   ____

4. What is the key point to stress?

   ____

   ____

THE USE OF THE SCRIPTURE IN CONVICTION
CHAPTER FOURTEEN

<u>QUESTIONS:</u>

1. What are the three skillful uses of the scripture in bringing conviction or sin to counselees?

    a.____

    ____

    b.____

    ____

    c.____

    ____

2. Conviction must be bypassed. [   ] True [   ] False
3. When should parables be used and take place?

    ____

    ____

    ____

    ____

SUPPLEMENTARY THOUGHTS
ABOUT CONVICTION
CHAPTER FIFTEEN

<u>QUESTIONS:</u>

1. What is the four step Biblical process of change outlined by Paul?

   a.____

   b. ____

   c. ____

   d. ____

2. God tells us to look for what in a changed lifestyle?

   ____

   ____

3. To be a faithful servant of Christ you must tell what you find as a counselor in a person even if that is not very complementary.
   [   ] True [   ] False

WHAT IS CONVICTION?
CHAPTER SIXTEEN

<u>QUESTIONS:</u>

1. What does 2 Timothy 3:16 say about the Greek word Epanorthosis?

   ____

   ____

2. What does correction mean in modern Greek?

   ____

   ____

3. Epanorthosis is used only here in the New Testament.
   [   ] True [   ] False

4. What is the purpose of feedback?

   ____

   ____

CORRECTION AND REPENTANCE
CHAPTER SEVENTEEN

<u>QUESTIONS:</u>

1. What does repent mean?

    ____

    ____

2. What is said about repentance in the King James Version that is misleading?

    ____

    ____

    ____

    ____

3. So what is repentance? And what does it encompass?

    ____

    ____

    ____

    a. ____
    b. ____
    c. ____
    d. ____

4. Correction is what point of change?

    ____

    ____

5. Is correction God's way of telling us stay down, brushing us off, turning us around and giving us a shove in the wrong direction. Yes or No. Explain.

    ____

    ____

CONFESSION OF SIN AND FORGIVENESS
CHAPTER EIGHTEEN

<u>QUESTIONS:</u>

1. What are the pivotal terms?

   ____

   ____

2. According to the Old Testament what does the word "yedah" mean?

   ____

   ____

3. What is the idea word behind confession?

   ____

   ____

4. What does the New Testament term Homlogeo or in more intensive form Exomologeo means?

   ____

   ____

5. Is confession a critical element in the process of change?
   [   ] Yes [   ] No

6. Without confession what happens?

   ____

   ____

7. How can a counselor help a person build a relationship with God?

   ____

   ____

8. Does God forgive sins? [   ] Yes [   ] No

FORSAKING SIN
CHAPTER NINETEEN

QUESTIONS:

1. Why should you be thankful that here is so much failure?

   ____

   ____

2. What does the Hebrew word Tsalesch means?

   ____

   ____

3. What happens to a person who holds on to sin?

   ____

   ____

4. Putting off sin includes the following:

   a. ____

   ____

   b. ____

   ____

   c. ____

   ____

5. There is one substitute for forsaking sin? [   ] Yes [   ] No

QUESTIONS:

1. How does one go about restoring an offender so that the situation is fully "corrected" and the member is able to "stand up straight again"?

   ____

   ____

2. What are the requirements that are explained in 2 Corinthians 2:6-11 about restoration?

   a. ____

   ____

   b. ____

   ____

   c. ____

   ____

3. Why should correction be treated as a matter of great importance?

   ____

   ____

4. What must a counselor do to help a sinner?

   ____

   ____

THE NEED FOR DISCIPLINED TRAINING IN RIGHTEOUSNESS
CHAPTER TWENTY-ONE

QUESTIONS:

1. What are the two sides of nature raising children?

   a. ____

   b. ____

2. What does Proverbs 29:15 say about the two-sided approach?

   ____

   ____

3. What is the Hebrew word for disciplined training? And its meaning?

   ____

   ____

4. Does forgiveness bring the guilt of the past? [   ] True [   ] False
5. When is change completed?

   ____

   ____

RIGHTEOUSNESS, THE GOAL
CHAPTER TWENTY-TWO

QUESTIONS:

1. In Luke 18:9, Paul quotes that the Jews rejected Christ because?

    ____

    ____

2. Which righteousness is acceptable to God?

    ____

    ____

3. What is the righteousness that comes by faith?

    ____

    ____

4. Is the righteousness of 2 Timothy 3:16 the same as the other righteousness mentioned in Romans 10:3, the righteousness that the Israelites tried to continue on their own?

    ____

    ____

5. What are the three kinds of righteousness Paul writes about?
    a. ____
    b. ____
    c. ____

6. What did Paul command in 2 Timothy 3:16?

    ____

    ____

7. The New Testament word for righteousness means?

    ____

    ____

8. The Old Testament word for righteousness means?

   ____

   ____

9. In what matter does Jesus want our righteousness to go and produce?

   ____

   ____

10. What was Peter looking forward to?

   ____

   ____

BUT IS RIGHTEOUSNESS POSSIBLE?
CHAPTER TWENTY-THREE

<u>QUESTIONS:</u>

1. What did God predict in Zachariah's prophetic hymn?

    ____

    ____

2. What two verses make it absolutely plain that we have been emancipated?

    ____

    ____

3. What is Peter saying in this verse? "It is not possible to live the remainder of your time in the flesh no longer following human desires but following the will of God."

    ____

    ____

4. How is the righteous life to be carried on?

    ____

    ____

5. Peter and Paul makes it clear that in order to live properly and struggle successfully against sin, one must do what?

    ____

    ____

6. How can a Christian cry out with sorrow and remorse?

    ____

    ____

7. What kind of trouble did Paul have and spoke about?

    ____

    ____

8. What did they say when Paul used the word body?

____

____

9. The word flesh is made over into what?

____

____

10. To walk in the flesh is to do what?

____

____

11. What is or why does Paul call the body death?

____

____

QUESTIONS:

1. What is the first factor in disciplining training in righteousness?

   ____

   ____

2. What is the first matter of importance that a counselor should know?

   ____

   ____

3. What are the two ways to look at a regenerated person?

   ____

   ____

4. Are we to become, in daily living, what we already are in Christ?
   [   ] Yes [   ] No

5. What is an important factor and deserves more attention in theology and Christian counseling?

   ____

   ____

6. Habit is a blessing from God that enables us to do what?

   ____

   ____

7. When dealing with habit it must be viewed as the work of what?

   ____

   ____

8. What changes is in the word ministered in the power of the Spirit?

____

____

9. What is another factor that should be mentioned in regards to rehabilitation?

____

____

10. What is the translator used for habit pattern in the Christian counselor's New Testament which have been quoted?

____

____

CONCLUSION
CHAPTER TWENTY-FIVE

<u>QUESTIONS:</u>

1. If and when you can't find an answer do or would you look elsewhere, in counseling where might you look for answers?

   ____

   ____

   ____

   ____

2. What is the most important thing you can do when counseling others?

   ____

   ____

   ____

   ____

3. The Christian Counselor must be a what?

   ____

   ____

   ____

   ____

PASTORAL COUNSELING

TEXTBOOK:
COMPETENT TO COUNSEL
BY JAY E. ADAMS

Approved By: Date: Approved By: Date:

___________________________   ___________________________

CHANCELLOR   *VERCHER*

"Study to Show Thyself Approved." 2 Timothy 2:15

PASTORAL COUNSELING   4 CREDIT HOURS

TEXTBOOK: COMPETENT TO COUNSEL
AUTHOR: JAY E. ADAMS
PUBLISHER: BAKER BOOK HOUSE

SUPPLIMENTAL RESOURCE MATERIAL:
    EFFECTIVE BIBLICAL COUNSELING
       AUTHOR: LAWRENCE L. CRABB, JR. / PUBLISHER: ZONDERVAN
    DR. JAMES DOBSON ANSWERS YOUR QUESTIONS
       AUTHOR: JAMES DOBSON / PUBLISHER: TYNDALE
    PROMISES
       AUTHOR: BILL BRIGHT / PUBLISHER: HERE'S A LIFE
    BUILDING UP ONE ANOTHER
       AUTHOR: GENE A GETZ / PUBLISHER: VICTOR BOOKS

THE BOOK COMPETENT TO COUNSEL WILL BE THE BASIC
TEXT. OTHER SUPPLEMENTAL MATERIAL WILL BE REFERRED
TO AS THE COURSE PROGRESSES.

STUDENTS WILL BE EXPECTED TO READ EACH CHAPTER AND
DO THE EXERCISES IN THE COURSE OUTLINE BY ANSWERING
ALL THE QUESTIONS AND FOREWARDING THE ANSWERS TO
THE TEACHER FOR GRADING AND TEACHER COMMENTS.

IF ADDITIONAL PAPER IS NEEDED IS NEEDED TO COMPLETE
THE ANSWERS PLEASE NOTE THE SUBJECT AND PAGE THE
ANSWERS ARE PERTAINING TO.

1ˢᵀ CLASS SESSION

Read the first chapter in text "COMPETENT TO COUNSEL"

After reading the first chapter refer to the study guide and answer the listed and prescribed questions.

CHAPTER 1	CHRISTIANITY AND PSYCHIATRY TODAY
Question 1	List the five things you can do for a person who is in a mental state of disturbance. Page 9 of text.
Question 2	Why is the usual religious approach not a good solution to the problem? What should the counselors try to do for those who come for counsel?
Question 3	Explain the meaning of the term "ID". Explain the meaning of the term "SUPEREGO". When does a conflict occur?
Question 4	Explain the difference between "EGO" functions and the function of the "ID" and "SUPEREGO". How can wee describe guilt feelings in relation to the "ID" and "SUPEREGO"?
Question 5	What should a counselor try to do when he tries to help a counselee?
Question 6	Name the different objectives between the counseling offered by a clergyman and a psychiatrist.
Question 7	What does the term "Psychological guilt" refer to? (Answer pg. 14)
Question 8	Explain Freud's attitude about Christianity. Explain his concept of Religion.
Question 9	State briefly the theory behind the author's views as he wrote the text "COMPETENT TO COUNSEL".

CHAPTER 2   THE HOLY SPIRIT AND COUNSELING
Read Chapter 2 in textbook.

Question 1   Explain in your own words as you answer the
                  following questions.

                  What is necessary for effective Christian counseling?

                  Make a list of some fundamental goals for a
                  Christian counselor.

                  What is the term that frequently is used in the
                  scriptures to describe these goals?

Question 2   What should be one of the main purposes for
                  Christian counseling?

Question 3   What should be the source of all Christian
                  counseling?

Question 4   What are we referring to when we talk about the
                  Holy Spirit?

Question 5   Describe the workings of the Holy Spirit.

Question 6   What resource is a Christian counselor to use to add
                  to his effective Christian counseling?

Question 7   What is one of the main differences between an
                  effective Christian counselor and a qualified
                  counselor who has acquired many necessary skills
                  in counseling but is not motivated by Christ?

CHAPTER 3   WHAT IS WRONG WITH THE MENTALLY ILL?

Read Chapter 3 in textbook.

Question 1   After reading the chapter; tell in your own words by writing a paragraph or less what you understand mental illness is.

Question 2   Describe the meaning of Homosexuality.

Question 3   Give a definition for the word "Psychiatric".

Question 4   Why should a Christian counselor cooperate (work) with a trained Christian Doctor?

Question 5   What is the one phrase referring to a term that needs to be removed from our conversation when referring to individuals who are suffering with emotional problems?

CHAPTER 4   WHAT IS NOUTHETIC COUNSELING?

Read Chapter 4 in the textbook.

Question 1   After you have read the chapter; explain what is mean
                    by "Nouthetic Counseling"?

                    Why should Nouthetic counseling be practiced by
                    Christians and Christian counselors in what counseling
                    they do along with relationships with others?

Question 2   What is the meaning of the word "DIDASKO"?

Question 3   What do the words imply as to actions that need to
                    take place when we refer to "Nouthetic Counseling"?

Question 4   How are we to counsel others if we are using
                    "Nouthetic Counseling"?

Question 5   List two reasons why counselors frequently fail?

Question 6   List a minimum of five requirements that are
                    necessary for a Christian counselor to have if he/she
                    is to experience success in the counseling that is done
                    with the counselee?

CHAPTER 5   THE PASTOR AS A NOUTHELETIC COUNSELOR

Read Chapter 5 in the textbook.

As you read this chapter make notes or underline the areas in your text that describes the duties of a Pastor when he is serving others in the areas of Noutheticing counseling.

Go back over your notes and write a summary of the chapter dealing with the subjects of Evangelism and Counseling, Nouthetic Counseling, Sanctification and the Pastor as a Counselor. Submit this summary for evaluation to the teacher along with answers to the questions on the other chapters of the text.

CHAPTER 6   NOUTHETIC   AND   ROGERIAN
COUNSELING

Read Chapter 6 in the textbook.

Question 1   List the many things a counselor must be willing
                    to do if he wants to be an effective counselor as
                    mentioned by Stanley Anderson in chapter 6.

Question 2   Is it possible to change a personality by giving
                    advice?

Question 3   What is the basic supposition about man as stated
                    by Carl Rogers?

Question 4   Why should conservative Christian counselors
                    reject the Rogerian theories?

Question 5   Is it proper to make judgments when counseling?

                    What does the author of the text say?

Question 6   List some of the techniques mentioned that are
                    necessary for effective directive counseling?

Question 7   What are the differences between the theories of
                    counseling expressed by Rogers and the counselor
                    who uses the bible?

CHAPTER 7   CONFESS YOUR SINS

Read Chapter 7 in the textbook.

Question 1	Describe "Hamartiagenic sickness".
	Give references from the Bible where James implies that sickness comes from sin.
Question 2	What are two sources for sickness that the author of James recognizes?
Question 3	What is said by the "Westminister Confession Faith" about the confessing of ones sins?
Question 4	Explain the thought that James expresses about the use of oil in his writings in the Bible. (it in mentioned on page 108 in the text.)
Question 5	List five things that a person should do when he/she is wiling to seek a healing through confession.
Question 6	Who is the first person a confession should be made to?
Question 7	In a brief account, describe what the author says about "MINIMIZING SIN".
	State how the author of the text suggests one should proceed when they are seeking help.
Question 8	Read the 32nd chapter of the book of Psalms and then state in your own words what David is saying is the source of all happiness.
Question 9	What is your definition of depression?
Question 10	For confession to be meaningful, what act must the counselee do after the confession has been made?
Question 11	What is one of the most meaningful experiences that the counselee is likely to have after they have experienced a real forgiveness?

CHAPTER 8   SOLVING PROBLEMS NOUTHETICALLY

Read chapter 8 in the textbook.

Question 1   Outline the chapter as you deal specifically with the following subjects.

Man's basic problem.

Why the words, "I can't" are not to be a part of Nouthetic counseling.

What do we mean when we say, "Counseling is giving hope"?

Question 2   List the three dimensions of problems and describe them.

Question 3   Why is building a life to be a part of Nouthetic counseling?

Question 4   Discuss the author's comments about problem solving through modeling, industry and institutionalization and child training.

CHAPTER 9   SOME PRINCIPLES OF NOUTHETIC
              TECHNIQUE

Read chapter 9 in the textbook.

Question 1   What is the hoped for objective of Nouthetic counseling?

Question 2   When using Nouthetic counseling methods in counseling, what is one of the major dangers that may occur and how should it be handled?

Question 3   Read chapter 12 of the book of Hebrews in the Bible and summarize briefly what this chapter is saying concerning discipline?

Question 4   When counselors try to lead counselees in the solving of problems, what are the things that may occur that can be helpful to the individual? What is being concealed?

Question 5   What is one of the first things a counselor should try to do in leading the client in doing before the next counseling session?

Question 6   After the first counseling session, should there be any special assignment given for the counselee (client) to do before the next meeting with the counselor?

Question 7   Explain the necessity for goal setting and how it can be done.

Question 8   When counseling, what must a counselor be careful that he not do?

Question 9   Explain why a counselor must deal with primary problems but must also always be aware of clues that will lead to the source of many problems that the client is trying to deal with.

Question 10   List some of the advantages of team counseling.

Question 11   Why is it undesirable for one counselor to give information about a client to another counselor privately when you are following Nouthetic counseling procedures?

Question 12   Explain what is meant by "Non-verbal Communication".

CHAPTER 10   COMMUNICATION AND MULTIPLE
               COUNSELING

Read Chapter 10 in the textbook.

Question 1   What is the present problem as it relates to
                  Communication and Counseling?

Question 2   What is God's solution for His Church?

Question 3   How should we deal with anger and resentment?

Question 4   What is meant when we say, "attack the problem
                  and not the people"?

Question 5   What should we consider doing if only one person
                  comes when the counseling session was arranged
                  for two people?

CHAPTER 11   CHRISTIAN   SCHOOL   TEACHERS   AS
NOUTHETIC COUNSELORS

Read chapter 11 in the textbook

Get the complete view of the subject the author is presenting before you look at any of the following questions.

Question 1   What is the assumption the author states should be recognized first before dealing with problems related to teacher/pupil relationships?

Question 2   Where are the three areas where problems will arise in a child's experience?

Question 3   What is the basic purpose for counseling in a Christian school environment?

Question 4   What is the major task of every Christian school teacher?

Question 5   Counseling principles can be conveyed best when they are taught in the form of living demonstrations. List the three things a Christian teacher should be aware or in his/her relationships with the pupils.

Question 6   Explain three of the most important considerations a school board should consider before they hire a teacher for the school.

Question 7   List ways God may use a teacher and then explain what the word "MATURATION" means as it pertains to education.

Question 8   The author deals with the problem of "INTERPERSONAL RELATIONS IN THE CLASSROOM". State the reasons for the principles and then explain why they should be followed by all teachers when problems arise.

Question 9   Who should be at the center of all Christian counseling?

Question 10   As your concluding exercise, please write a brief evaluation of this course.

PREMARITAL COUNSELING

TEXTBOOK:
MARRIAGE COUNSELING
BY H. NORMAN WRIGHT

Approved By:　　　　Date:　　　　Approved By:　　　　Date:

CHANCELLOR　　　　　　　*VERCHER*

"Study to Show Thyself Approved." 2 Timothy 2:15

PREMARITAL COUNSELING   8 CREDIT HOURS

TEXTBOOK: MARRIAGE COUNSELING
AUTHOR: H. NORMAN WRIGHT

THE PURPOSE OF THIS COURSE IS TO AID THE COUPLE TOWARDS A SOLUTION FROM CRITICAL PROBLEMS THAT MAY ARISE IN THE MARRIAGE. THIS COURSE OFFERS BIBLICAL PRINCIPLES AND PROVEN TECHNIQUES TO HELP THE COUPLE WORK THROUGH DIFFICULT ISSUES THAT ARE AFFECTING MANY MARRIAGES. IT IS RECOMMENDED THAT YOU READ THE ENTIRE TEXTBOOK. THROUGH MARRIAGE YOU WILL CONTINUE A LIFELONG JOURNEY OF HEALING AND GROWING TOGETHER.

STUDENTS WILL BE EXPECTED TO READ EACH CHAPTER AND DO THE EXERCISES IN THE COURSE OUTLINE BY ANSWERING ALL THE QUESTIONS AND FOREWARDING THE ANSWERS TO THE TEACHER FOR GRADING AND TEACHER COMMENTS.

IF ADDITIONAL PAPER IS NEEDED TO COMPLETE THE ANSWERS PLEASE NOTE THE SUBJECT AND PAGE THE ANSWERS ARE PERTAINING TO.

EXPECTATIONS THAT HAMPER THE MARRIAGE
CHAPTER ONE

QUESTIONS:

1. What are the expectations that hamper a marriage?

   ____

   ____

2. Can expectations evolve into demands? [   ] Yes [   ] No

NEED FULFILLMENT IS ESSENTIAL

1. What is essential for a person's satisfaction and development?

   ____

   ____

UNMET CHILDHOOD NEEDS AS A SOURCE OF CONFLICTS

1. What might unmet childhood needs include?

   ____

   ____

2. Love, security and belonging unmet needs may turn into what?

   ____

   ____

3. What are two examples of false needs?

   ____

   ____

UNMET NEEDS WITHIN MARRIAGE

1. What are the unmet needs within marriage?

   ____

   ____

THE BASIC NEEDS OF MEN AND WOMEN

1. Explain the five most basic needs in marriage for both men and women.
   b. Man____
   b. Woman_______________________________________

2. What is it called every time a spouse interacts with the partner they either make a deposit or a withdrawal?

   ____

   ____

OBJECTIONS TO EXPRESSING NEEDS

1. What are the three statements that typify reactions a counselor might hear?

   ____

   ____

VARIATIONS OF BEHAVIORAL APPROACHES
CHAPTER TWO

<u>QUESTIONS:</u>

1. What are the predictable patterns of behavior that couples will engage in?

   ____

   ____

2. What approach can you take?

   ____

   ____

3. How many steps can a couple take to have the opportunity to begin to challenge the negative beliefs they have about each other?

   ____

   ____

INTERVENTION

1. List the five step approach by Richard Stuart

   ___________________   ___________________

   ___________________   ___________________

   ____

BEHAVIORAL – EXCHANGE PROGRAM

1. What is the five step method based upon reciprocal exchange and behavior modification within the marriage?

   ___________________   ___________________

   ___________________   ___________________

   ____

1. What is a positive reinforcement?

    ____

    ____

2. Is it <u>common</u> or <u>uncommon</u> for a couple to work out an actual written contract concerning their positive behaviors?

    ____

    ____

3. What happens to a possessive and insecure person?

    ____

    ____

4. What is the "please" approach?

    ____

    ____

5. What are the three categories that the negotiator role involves assisting each party to obtain what they want?

    ____

    ____

THE COGNITIVE APPROACH TO
MARRIAGE COUNSELING
CHAPTER THREE

QUESTIONS:

1. What are the four steps in the process in cognitive counseling or therapy?

   _______________________   _______________________

   _______________________   _______________________

2. What are the several steps that are necessary in self-talk?

   ____

   ____

3. What are some of the dictionary statements of self-talk?

   ____

   ____

4. What are the steps to overcome negative talk?

   ____

   ____

5. What are the five methods of reinforcing and clarifying self-talk?

   _______________________   _______________________

   _______________________   _______________________

   ____

6. What are the four areas, suggested by Dr. Everett Worthington Jr. and Douglas McMurry?

   _______________________   _______________________

   _______________________   _______________________

7. What five steps did Dr. Worthington and Pastor McMurry
   suggest to changing the destructive assumptions?

   a.____

   ____

   b.____

   ____

   c.____

   ____

   d.____

   ____

   e.____

   ____

8. What are the three counselors roles in clarifying behavioral
   patterns?

   ____

   ____

VARIATIONS WITHIN THE COUNSELING SESSION
CHAPTER FOUR

FACTORS THAT DETERMINE STRUCTURE

<u>QUESTIONS:</u>

1. What are the several factors that determine structure?

____

____

____

____

2. What are the two ways to resolve problems of who is to set the rules?

_____________________________   _____________________________

COUPLES IN CONFLICT
CHAPTER FIVE

MARITAL CONFLICT IS NORMAL

QUESTIONS:

1. Is conflict in a marriage normal? [   ] Yes [   ] No
2. Define the word conflict.

____

____

CONFLICT PATTERNS

1. Write out the five basic styles or methods. Then draw a model explaining them.
   a.______________________________
   b. ______________________________
   c. ______________________________
   d. ______________________________
   e. ______________________________

FIVE CONFLICT STYLES
STRATEGIES AND RESULTING INTERACTION

1. What are the two strategies that guide the response to conflict?

_____________________   _____________________

ALTERNATIVES FOR RESOLVING CONFLICT

1. What are the guidelines or handling disagreements?

    ____

    ____

2. What are the four illustrated suggestive so couples can understand each other?

    ____________________   ____________________

    ____________________   ____________________

3. What are the four important questions couples need to meet together? And discuss?

    ____________________   ____________________

    ____________________   ____________________

4. What are the six stages or problem solving

    ____________________   ____________________

    ____________________   ____________________

    ____________________   ____________________

CONFLICT AND ABUSIVENESS

1. What are the four kinds of abuse identified in 1974 when Congress passed the child abuse prevention and treatment act?

    ____________________   ____________________

    ____________________   ____________________

THE PATTERN OF ABUSE

1. List the pattern of abuse.

    ____

    ____

1. What following steps must be taken to help an abused person?

   ____

   ____

AN ANGER-REDUCTION APPROACH

1. What are seven steps to assist abusive or angry spouses?

   a. ____

   b. ____

   c. ____

   d. ____

   e. ____

   f. ____

   g. ____

2. What are the three causes of anger?

   ____

   ____

3. Blame is a relationship crippler. [   ] True [   ] False

HOW TO REBUILD COMMUNICATION
IN MARRIAGE
CHAPTER SIX

<u>QUESTIONS:</u>

1. By who are the two articles illustrated the various styles of assisting couples in rebuilding their communication?

   ____

   ____

2. What are the procedures to use in the counseling session?

   ____

   ____

3. What are the six communication steps?

   a. ____
   b. ____
   c. ____
   d. ____
   e. ____
   f. ____

4. What are the methods of getting rid of anger and resentment?

   ____

   ____

DEVELOP POSITIVE FEELINGS TOWARD
THE RESENTED PERSON

1. What is the one final step that is a necessary part of releasing resentment?

   ____

   ____

THE AFFAIR
CHAPTER SEVEN

<u>QUESTIONS:</u>

1. What does fidelity in a marriage mean?

   ____

   ____

2. What is fidelity?

   ____

   ____

3. Many affairs occur for only one reason. [   ] True [   ] False
4. During mid-life, affairs are common. [   ] True [   ] False
5. What are the other reasons for having an affair described by Dwight Small?

   ______________________   ______________________

   ______________________   ______________________

   ______________________   ______________________

   ______________________   ______________________

6. What are the three R's of infidelity?

   ______________________   ______________________

   ____

7. What are Carder's three varieties of affairs?

   ______________________   ______________________

   ____

8. What are Braun's five varieties of affairs?

   a. ____

   b. ____

   c. ____

   d. ____

   e. ____

9. What are the three basic patterns that occur when a person chooses to terminate an affair?

____

____

10. Effects of an affair upon a marriage are?

____

____

11. Should the offended person be told about the affair? Should they confess?

____

____

12. What are the infidel's curves that are divided into four phases?
    Phase 1_______________________________________
    Phase 2_______________________________________
    Phase 3_______________________________________
    Phase 4_______________________________________

13. What are the spouse's curves that are divided into four phases?
    Phase 1_______________________________________
    Phase 2_______________________________________
    Phase 3_______________________________________
    Phase 4_______________________________________

14. Warning signs by people who have had an affair, what are they?
    a. ____
    b. ____
    c. ____
    d. ____

PITFALLS IN COUNSELING
CHAPTER EIGHT

<u>QUESTIONS:</u>

1. What are the potential counseling problems?

    a. ____
    b. ____
    c. ____
    d. ____
    e. ____
    f. ____
    g. ____
    h. ____
    i. ____
    j. ____
    k. ____
    l. ____
    m. ____
    n. ____
    o. ____
    p. ____

2. What can be done with resistances?
    First____
    Second____
    Third____
    Fourth____

3. Do Couples need confidence? [   ] Yes [   ] No
4. Is it important for a counselor to know and discuss couples sexual matters?
    [   ] Yes [   ] No

MODELING JESUS' COUNSELING METHOD

1. What was "Jesus' style of relating"?

   a. ____

   b. ____

   c. ____

   d. ____

   e. ____

   f. ____

IN CONCLUSION

1. What is counseling and what is our task as counselors?

   ____

   ____

   ____

   ____

APPEDIX 1

1. What are the four cautions in presenting the results of T-JTA?

   a.____

   ____

   b.____

   ____

   c.____

   ____

   d.____

   ____

APPENDIX 2

<u>QUESTIONS:</u>

1. What are the seven important skills for couples?

    a. ____

    b. ____

    c. ____

    d. ____

    e. ____

    f. ____

    g. ____

WHAT HAPPENS TO MARRIAGES
CHAPTER NINE

QUESTIONS:

1. What is said in Matthew 7:26 about a house built on sand reflecting on marriages?

____

____

2. What happens to an unplanned marriage?

____

____

3. What happens to marriages built on dreams?

____

____

4. What are the two basic causes for trouble in marriage?

____

____

5. Most couples expect three things from their marriage, what are they?

____

____

AFTER THE HONEYMOON

1. What do married couples need to understand after the honeymoon?

____

____

____

____

____

2. What are some of the other different expectations that are listed?

    a. ____

    b. ____

    c. ____

    d. ____

    e. ____

    f. ____

MARRIAGE TODAY

1. The first year of marriage by Miriam Around and Samuel Parker is what?

    ____

    ____

2. Explain: A strong and week foundation of marriage.

    ____

    ____

UNSATISFACTORY MARITAL BEHAVIOR PATTERNS

1. List some of the unsatisfactory marital behaviors.

    a. ____

    b. ____

    c. ____

    d. ____

    e. ____

    f. ____

MARITAL SATISFACTION FLUCTUATES DURING THE FAMILY LIFE CYCLE

1. What are some of the created problems couples begin to have in a family cycle?

    a. ____

    b. ____

c. ____

d. ____

2. What is identity?

____

____

3. What is intimacy?

____

____

CHILD REARING

1. Why is parenting a crisis time for many married couples?

____

____

THE MIDDLE YEARS OF MARRIAGE

1. What happens during the middle years of marriage?

____

____

2. Explain, "Men in mid-life crisis".

____

____

RETIREMENT

1. What is one of the greatest struggles in retirement?

____

____

2. During retirement some people do not know what to do with themselves.

[   ] True [   ] False

A BIBLICAL PERSPECTIVE OF COUNSELING
CHAPTER TEN

CHARACTERISTICS OF JESUS APPROACH TO COUNSELING

QUESTIONS:

1. The way Jesus ministered to others is a model for all who counsel.
   [   ] True [   ] False

2. Jesus' counseling approach was done by appointment and just in a few minutes.
   [   ] True [   ] False

3. What kind of approaches did Jesus use and where do we find them in the Bible?

   a. ____
   b. ____
   c. ____
   d. ____

4. How did Jesus give worth? And what was his priority?

   ____

   ____

SAID THE RIGHT WORDS

1. How did Jesus speak?

   ____

   ____

EMPHASIZED RIGHT BEHAVIOR

1. What book can you find Jesus emphasizing the right in the lives of those to whom he ministered?

    ____

    ____

SOUGHT TO HAVE PEOPLE ACCEPT RESPONSIBILITY

1. In what way did Jesus seek to have the man accept responsibility? What was Jesus' response?

    a.____

    ____

    b.____

    ____

GAVE HOPE

1. What was some of Jesus' approaches he used on people?

    ____

    ____

2. What chapter gave an example of Jesus admonished and confronted?

    ____

    ____

BIBLICAL PERSPECTIVES IN A SECULAR MODEL

1. What are the five steps suggested by Egan and Brammar illustrated in the Bible for counseling?

    a. ____

    b. ____

    c. ____

    d. ____

    e. ____

2. What were the techniques Jesus used to help the two men with their crisis and period of discouragement?

a. ____

b. ____

c. ____

d. ____

e. ____

f. ____

FACTORS IN THE EFFECTIVENESS OF JESUS' MINISTRY

1. Why was Jesus so effective in his ministry?

BIBLICAL PRINCIPLES OF COUNSELING

1. What should we do or say in a counseling situation when we are forced as Christian counselors to ask, "Lord, what should I do now? What does this person need?"

a. ____

b. ____

c. ____

d. ____

e. ____

f. ____

g. ____

h. ____

i. ____

j. ____

k. ____

2. What are the principles of counseling?

a. ____

b. ____

c. ____

d. ____

THE COUNSELOR'S ROLE IN WORKING WITH THE MARITAL COUPLE
CHAPTER ELEVEN

MAKING COUNSELING DECISIONS

QUESTIONS:

1. What are some of the reasons referrals are made?

    a. ____

    b. ____

    c. ____

2. What are the four kinds of sessions?

    a. ____

    b. ____

    c. ____

    d. ____

3. Give an example for Verbatim account from a counseling session.

    ____

    ____

THE COUNSELORS PROFILE

1. Give the five paramount roles we must provide.

    a. ____

    b. ____

    c. ____

    d. ____

    e. ____

PREFERENCE ALTERNATIVE PRINCIPLES

1. List four pairs of preference alternatives.

    a. ____

b. ____

c. ____

d. ____

THE PEOPLE PUZZLE

1. What book and by whom will you find this sentence? "Human beings are particularly driven by early deficit in their lives."

BABY BOOMER AWARENESS

1. What is the definition for a "Baby Boomer"?
2. What are the four E's the baby boomers have been characterized by?

   a. ____

   b. ____

   c. ____

   d. ____